INVOCATION:

"Too hard 'twill be to satirize,
For the times they are so queer."
To which Good Sir Branklin quick replies,
"Holdith my beer!"

WOKE RICHARD'S ALMANACK

Being the choicest Morsels of Wisdom

(Or approximation somewhat thereof)

written in the year of the Almanack's publication

by Mr. Fenjamin Branklin of Charles Towne.

The significantly more obscure successor

to our well-renowned savant.

CREEKSIDE
Publishing House

© 2025 Clay Tucker
All Rights Reserved.

ISBN: 979-8-9986375-5-1

Creekside Publishing House
Over yonder
Goat Island, SC

Courteous Reader,

It would seem hardly necessary to state,
though not much can be deemed obvious
in our current day, that the authorship
of these herein maxims and aphorisms
are ascribed to a nom-de-plume,
of which there is no relation
to the spoonerized* namesake.
Though they may be of kindred spirit
in the pursuit of the mother wit.

Clay Tucker
Editor

---

*A Spoonerism is the verbal error in which
the first letter or sound of two words are transposed.
And you didn't think you would learn anything!

<u>NOTE:</u>

To make the predecessor proud,
This endeavour begins by
laying out a set of virtues.
As well as leaving
The "u" in endeavour.

THE THIRTEEN VIRTUES OF THE LEFT

1. Identity
2. Audacity
3. Blame
4. Ingratitude
5. Incompetence
6. Blame
7. Deception
8. Destruction
9. Delusion
10. Blame
11. Vanity
12. Promiscuity
13. Blame

THE MANY MAXIMS
OF THE LEFT

Henceforth the all-new dictum,
That the victor shalt be the victim.

The policy priority be trickle-down authority.

Thou shalt tell the narrative, the whole narrative,
And nothing but the narrative.

Play the masses like a fiddle,
As ye feign to tackith to the middle.

Stifle the rumour that thou art a groomer.

Fret not when'er thee fail,
For upward ye will surely sail!

Do not stress, ye have the press.

The older to their ways are clung,
So better get the voter young!

In unison we shall all pronounce,
That, actually, 'twas a Republican pounce!

From each according to their gullibility.

The problem is the solution,
For perpetual revolution.

Applause and adoration for overregulation.

Though thou knowith it doth not exist,
Add "democratic" ahead of socialist.

If thee lackith support,
Then packith the court!

Avoidith candor, simply pander.

If "public union" sounds like jargon,
Try it out, it's quite a bargain!

Maketh flirtations with reparations.

It matters not if they dissent,
Use heavy hand of government!

───────────────

The taste is naught but honey,
When using other people's money.

If they're to thy right, ye must gaslight!

Three things that art a perfect fusion,
Diversity, Equity, and Inclusion.

Erodeth the foundation of Western Civilization.

Rejoice! Rejoice! Polls swing pro-choice.
Tis great the unborn have no voice!

───────────────

Thou shalt never be remiss
To add a word before justice.

If they sniggered then say you're triggered.

Don't be kind to neighbors,
Lest they start to ask for favors.

See it all through prism of rampant corporatism.

If thou cannot blame thy race,
Then settle in for second place.

One thing under our control,
Is just how far we shift the goal.

Set thy sights on the Bill of Rights!

In the DNC opportunity knocks,
If thee checkith off a box.

Take no abstention from market intervention.

If thee deem there is a flaw,
Simply don't enforce the law!

On this matter do not tarry,
Maketh thy city a sanctuary!

Maketh laws conducive to being more intrusive.

I knowith not exactly where,
But sureth the buck stopith there.

Let there be no ending to our frivolously spending!

Do not bluster as we muster
To do away with filibuster.

Henceforth beside the bust,
Each coin shalt read, "In Gov. We Trust."

To please the base, choose freshest face!

As the rich get richer,
So shalt the bitchy get bitchier.

Thou art noble and special for ye participated.

Ye needn't pass a close inspection,
So long as ye meet intersection.

Make all terms a little muddy,
And callith it a social study.

Speak truth to power on the hour.

Promise perks at every rally,
And watch the votes begin to tally.

Make thy niche the bait and switch.

To those just beginning,
Never stopith spinning!

A golden age is soon upon us,
Twas said before but now I promise.

Well said is better than well done.

It matters not but larger goal,
If winning office means losing soul.

Let no tragedy go to waste. Even if thou caused it.

One thing that sets our hearts aflame
Is finding where to place the blame.

Let no transgression be cause for schism.
We'll all say we hate it and give it an -ism.

Do not hide a fault. Declare it merit and exalt!

Though it may seem insurmountable,
Never hold thyself accountable.

Tis only rational to maketh all things national.

At thy disposal the special forces,
That goith by name of anonymous sources.

To have success, increase largesse!

Don't stop or even second guess,
To prejudge those of prejudice.

Young Sylvia taught first grade,
And by and large the children obeyed.
Though on occasion had some confusion,
As she bounced from equity to inclusion.
And the parents balked when they found out,
But as it stood, they had no clout.
So Sylvia plugged away, of course,
Changing minds at the source!

If your style be a bit taboo,
Just change the world to mimic you!

Don't let morals deter your passion,
Let them come and go like fashion.

Huff and puff and say that it's not far enough.

Let it be to thy delight,
That we've expanded oversight.

Keep thy grip on censorship!

Thou chooseth what be worse to thee,
Adulting or adultery.

For your approval we submit,
To blowith out the deficit.

Our comfort foods art platitudes.

If thou cannot win then cheat,
And if thou cannot cheat then quit.

A lifelong goal, be on the dole!

Be wary, for once ye start restricting
It may indeed become addicting.

Support the cause without a pause,
And then receive a round applause.

When in doubt, don't stop just shout!

Wear thy virtue on thy sleeve,
Whether or not ye truly believe.

God bless the IRS!

Of this accord don't screw the pooch,
Divine always to be a mooch!

Never mind the need or size,
What'er thee can, subsidize!

Report. Then verify.

When it comes to history be excitable,
That where it's stored is quite rewritable.

Protect our infiltration of public education.

Whether long or shorter range,
Thy aim shalt be for sweeping change.

Ye shalt be on an endless quest,
To findith something to protest.

Thou can't deny, Duty is a four-letter word.

Thou shalt always be steering
For social engineering.

If they inspect, misdirect!

If ye liketh not a question,
Dubith it microaggression.

One small snip for man,
One pliant sheep for transkind.

To be subjective is the objective!

Question not if narcissistic,
Each person shalt be atomistic.

Be forever bending to what ye see is trending.

First thing in the mornings,
Cry out all thy trigger warnings.

If at first ye don't have it both ways,
Try, try again.

A man of straw is our Shangri-La.

It should come as no surprise
To find what ye can weaponize.

The utmost task, don't slip the mask!

Set the content out to pasture,
For the message is the master.

It shall be posh to have brainwash.

Thy principals will forever last,
Ye shout whilst tearing down the past.

The widow Doris sang in the chorus.
Her singing was fine but her talking would bore us.
For on every subject she had an opinion,
Whether or not it was in her dominion.
Which was, I think, naught but a baker,
Though that little fact did little to shake her.
She insisted, always, that she was correct,
Though I think, on the facts, she seldom did check.

Let us clearith off the slate,
To maketh all new nanny state!

We've reached the crest. We've seen the best.
So tax it to hell and distribute the rest.

Envy is the new flattery.

If to a rural town ye goes,
Thou shalt lookith down thy nose.

Use any stage to show thy rage.

How marvelous the glory
Of making all things mandatory!

Tis an honored tradition to switch thy position.

It shall be our greatest trick
To always blame their rhetoric.

Buckrum was a happy lad,
But sourcing food had made him sad.
He thought there was a better way,
So this is what he had to say.
"Let's capith off the quantity,
Where our stock can roam and wander free,
And when the masses start to plea,
I'm sure we'll feed them magically."

It matters not what's yours or mine,
The bread's so good we stand in line!

Let me make this crystal clear,
Tell them what they want to hear.

An idol be the idle free.

If ye wish to gain an edge,
There's nothing ye cannot allege!

Never narc upon earmark.

There is no need to question why,
When we've putith experts up on high.

Show nothing short of blind support!

No amount of facts should sway
Thy want to take their guns away.

Robin was close to her ideal life.
All that she needed was a wonderful wife.
So imagine the day that her girlfriend proposed,
But a few little things I should probably disclose.
They tended to fight more often than not,
And the paybacks, of course, were elaborate plots.
But never mind that, cause the lead's been buried,
For everything's perfect as soon as you're married!

When performing thy ablution,
Use U.S. Constitution!

Though the joke be good, we will not laugh.
In fact, we shalt be offended on thy behalf.

Giles Jolt went out with a bolt,
But nobody blinked for he was a dolt.
Caught with his hands in the proverbial jar.
What he had done, we agreed, was a little too far.
But the haste doth appear chock full of spite,
And is there a chance that it comes back to bite?
"No," they all say. "This must be the way."
So go on and cancel, cancel away!

Derangement ye shall receive on high,
For lo, the Orange-Man drawith nigh!

Let no one persuade thee,
no logic pervade thee,
no doubt to ensue thee,
nor shame to imbue thee,
for thou art stout in thy correctness,
and me in my directness,
that it all comes down to this,
thou shalt always live in bliss,
if other's views thy do dismiss.
Adieu.

THE END

WARNING!

*You are now entering the center.
It may appear empty, but that's only
'cause nothing is there.*

WARNING!

You are now entering the center.
It may appear empty, but that's only
'cause nothing is there.

Let no one persuade thee,
no logic pervade thee,
no doubt to ensue thee,
nor shame to imbue thee,
for thou art stout in thy correctness,
and me in my directness,
that it all comes down to this,
thou shalt always live in bliss,
if other's views thy do dismiss.
Adieu.

THE END

Out loud ye shan't acknowledge,
But say a prayer for electoral college.

Bossy Betty was mighty petty
As the largest local debtee.
Though what she did was not a crime,
It gave new meaning to nickel-and-dime.
An increase now and another one later.
Whether or not the renters would hate her.
So heed the lesson that she has lent,
And jack up all your tenets' rent!

Pretend that thou doth really care,
But giveth no more than thought and prayer.

Be someone who can extol
Each and every rabbit hole.

Time is money, or so they say,
But they are wrong in one big way.
Old friend Berryman works real hard,
So all that he has he's tempted to guard.
But little does our old friend know,
That money's quick to come and go.
Therefore money stacks to time just barely,
So donate often but volunteer rarely.

Among us all, the one's most pious
Art those most able to flaunt their bias.

Do not fear to be elated
If ye come across as antiquated.

Take a note, suppress the vote!

If thee suspect a hostile crowd,
Don't say the quiet part out loud.

Beith matrimonial to views that art colonial.

They will try, but can't destroy,
The club we call the good-old-boys.

Feel felicity with thy toxicity!

On thy last day in the White House Garden,
Don't forget to Pardon! Pardon! Pardon!

Justice is for just us.

Tis not an abnormality
To love a cultish personality.

When they poll, be a troll!

Say that thee are for the people,
But only those below the steeple.

Thou shalt not allow retorting
To our fair and balanced reporting.

Take no sabbatical from being radical.

Ye should pickith what to trim
By simply going on a whim.

Control thy salivation at inside information.

If they tellith thee to flip,
Then do not question leadership.

We will tout thee as divine,
So long ye help the bottom line.

Only traffic in thy demographic.

Are independents worth the chase,
When thou can countith on the base?

Ye shall conform to breaking norm.

Be vocal for the pro-life cause,
But abortith thine without a pause.

When it comes to truth, I think I'll judge,
There's nothing quite as sweet as fudge.

Have the gall to blame cabal.

Ye may have called for act of war,
But who is really keeping score?

Tis always season for minor treason!

Let it fill thy guts with bile
To even think of crossing aisle.

Take the time to bitch and moan,
When'er thee have a megaphone.

We shall call it haute if ye are rote.

The difference 'twixt good and great,
Tis whether thee can bloviate.

When ye exploit, be adroit!

Do not show a slight concern,
What'er thee can, overturn!

Try to hide thy raging boner,
Whilst talking with a wealthy doner.

Pick up the slack with super PAC!

At the top of thy appointment list,
Placeth nothing but a jingoist.

Light a votive for the profit motive.

We shalt maketh it a friendly game,
To always levy baseless claim.

If they wish for thee to show some spine,
We recommend ye just decline.

Ribbons and confetti to ye that beith petty.

Thy eye shall have a special glint,
When'er ye cut entitlement.

The party theme is to be extreme.

Pretend to bash, but we all know,
Ye love the dog and pony show.

Though it hits in great disparity,
Always call for more austerity.

Taketh stock in foreign hawk.

Imagine all the things at threat,
Once we have triumvirate.

We have the quorum to ditch decorum.

Go ahead with thy monopoly,
For they regulate it sloppily.

We shalt gauge thy rightness
Depending on thy whiteness.

Come along for the ride of national pride.

They say we art a melting pot,
But if you ask we'd rather not.

Keepith calm and discriminate on.

If substitution has ye leery,
Simply query replacement theory.

As first resort, just deport!

Take solace! Thou art not alone
If ye fearith the unknown.

To east and west we have the sea,
But ships may cross it easily.
To north we have supposed friend,
But will they be there to the end?
To south we have a constant flow,
But where will all those migrants go?
I thinkith we should block them all,
So round the country build a wall!

Greenlight the sequel
To separate but equal.

Thou wilt never foot the bill
If ye can be a corporate shill.

Be a pawn of the neo-con.

If the hate amongst the crowd is great,
Then do not wait to instigate!

Let thy disdain be very plain.

Greed is good thou oft opine.
Try avarice, it's quite divine!

Thou shalt study the encyclopedia
Of how to harass the media.

Let it shower corporate power.

If traditional marriage fails ye twice,
The third or fourth should soon suffice.

Ne'er look askance.at sycophants.

Expect no more than wink and nod,
When ye commitith act of fraud.

The workers won't have time to dawdle,
In our perfect business model.

Surgeon Sam was a generous man,
With a large income to spend.
He bought what he liked with plenty to spare,
So a hand he thought he'd lend.
By giving some to charities,
But this I must instruct,
When April middle rolls around,
Deduct! Deduct! Deduct!

Ye shall receive a hefty prize,
For everything ye privatize.

Pay all the taxes that ye owe,
But maketh sure the loopholes grow!

Rule number one, do no charm.

Let 'er ye do be at behest
Of good ole special interest.

Let us prep for locking step.

When thou art rich ye will feed the poor,
So said all the rich that came before.

Our special sauce is more chaos.

It shouldn't come as any shock,
That all we crave is more gridlock.

Make Fox News thy only muse.

Tis nothing gained from talking yoyos,
Let discourse go the way of dodos!

Putith the crass in democracy.

Admitith not that ye don't know,
Even when it clearly shows.

If audience doth start to bore,
just revert to culture war!

Take offense at common sense.

Henceforward, the party shall consist
Of naught but Christian nationalist.

Make provision for more division.

Thou should always be contented,
That we're overrepresented.

They may suspect what we all know,
We badly need the status quo!

Make genuine threat to the safety net.

Do not fear a bubble burst,
For the bailouts cometh our way first.

There's no debate, simply hate!

Showith not the slightest humor
If they startith chanting boomer.

We shalt label thee a pagan
If ye fail to worship Reagan.

Strike up the band for Ayn Rand!

As oft ye can ye must arrange
For yet another regime change.

Rude in the streets, prude in the sheets.

If ye wish thy fame to grow,
Putith on a circus show.

Analyze with single factor,
Will it help defense contractor?

Whimsical Will was feeling quite ill,
So the doctor prescribed an exorbitant pill.
It worked like a charm, got him back on the reg,
For the small little price of an arm and leg.
So he went on his way, but it wasn't too long,
'Fore the illness came back, and came back strong.
And the doctor said, "You're an unlucky chump,
For you'll double the cost and just be a stump."

Let's agree to disagree
On what we call reality.

Stand up straight in proud defiance,
Of what most doth simply callith science.

When in doubt, say, "What About?"

If ye lose then don't just stand there,
Help us while we gerrymander!

Repeatith like a parrot thy claim to value merit.

Do not let it ring alarms,
How much we love to bearith arms.

If it stokes, spread the hoax!

American made is what ye tout,
So here at home manufacture doubt.

Party like it's 1619.

Free speech we say is number one,
But banning books is so much fun!

Do not even sayith gay.

If thou partake of what ye claim forbidden,
Then, by God, at least try keep it hidden!

Be proud of thy creation,
Whether mis, or dis, or malinformation.

Let thy moral panic be organic.

Fearith not a swift dismissal,
For they cannot prove a doggie whistle.

Shoutith Yahtzee if thy follower's a Nazi.

Allowith no disruption
To the everyday corruption.

THE MANY MAXIMS

OF THE RIGHT

Do not leave thy bliss to chance,
Double down on ignorance!

Thou cannot spell patriotism without riot.

Keep the budget nice and lean.
Except, of course, the war machine.

THE THIRTEEN VIRTUES

OF THE RIGHT

1. Intolerance
2. Greed
3. Uniformity
4. Greed
5. Bigotry
6. Bellyache
7. Greed
8. Misogyny
9. Hypocrisy
10. Greed
11. Oppression
12. Obstruction
13. Greed

NOTE:

To make the predecessor proud,
This endeavour begins by
laying out a set of virtues.
As well as leaving
The "u" in endeavour.

Courteous Reader,

It would seem hardly necessary to state,
though not much can be deemed obvious
in our current day, that the authorship
of these herein maxims and aphorisms
are ascribed to a nom-de-plume,
of which there is no relation
to the spoonerized* namesake.
Though they may be of kindred spirit
in the pursuit of the mother wit.

Clay Tucker

Editor

**A Spoonerism is the verbal error in which
the first letter or sound of two words are transposed.
And you didn't think you would learn anything!*

© 2025 Clay Tucker
All Rights Reserved.

ISBN: 979-8-9986375-5-1

Creekside Publishing House
Over yonder
Goat Island, SC

MAGA RICHARD'S ALMANACK

Being the choicest Morsels of Wisdom
(Or approximation somewhat thereof)
written in the year of the Almanack's publication
by Mr. Fenjamin Branklin of Charles Towne.
The significantly more obscure successor
to our well-renowned savant.

CREEKSIDE
Publishing House

INVOCATION:

"Too hard 'twill be to satirize,
For the times they are so queer."
To which Good Sir Branklin quick replies,
"Holdith my beer!"

www.ingramcontent.com/pod-product-compliance
Lightning Source LLC
Chambersburg PA
CBHW050521100526
44581CB00002B/61